DOG

vs.

CAT

A Nation Divided

*Dirty Tricks and Other Shocking Secrets
from a Nasty Pet Election*

Don Asmussen

**Andrews McMeel
Publishing, LLC**
Kansas City

★DOG★
vs.
★CAT★
A Nation Divided

Don Asmussen's cartoon, *Bad Reporter*, is distributed
by Universal Press Syndicate and originated in the
San Francisco Chronicle.

The drawings inside used dog and cat heads
from the Dover Clip-Art series.

06 07 08 09 10 RR2 10 9 8 7 6 5 4 3 2 1

ISBN-13: 978-0-7407- 6191-1
ISBN-10: 0-7407- 6191-9

Library of Congress Catalog Control Number: 2006925700

www.andrewsmcmeel.com

ATTENTION: SCHOOLS AND BUSINESSES
Andrews McMeel books are available at quantity discounts
with bulk purchase for educational, business, or sales promo-
tional use. For information, please write to: Special Sales
Department, Andrews McMeel Publishing, LLC, 4520 Main
Street, Kansas City, Missouri 64111.

For my brother, Dean

"The vote was taken at once,
and it was agreed by an overwhelming
majority that rats were comrades.
There were only four dissentients,
the three dogs and the cat, who was afterwards
discovered to have voted on both sides."

—*Animal Farm*, George Orwell

TABLE OF
★ **CONTENTS** ★

★ A NOTE FROM THE AUTHOR ★

It has become more and more apparent over the last twenty years that divisiveness has poisoned our national debate. Nuanced discussion and compromise have been replaced by name-calling, bullying, and barely disguised hate speech.

Never has our country been so fractured in our history.

I am, of course, referring to the widening gulf separating dog lovers and cat lovers. Dog lovers, long a people steeped in the tradition of family values and strong home protection, have always been critical of cat lovers, who often come off as elitist, cold, finicky, and not in the least bit interested in our protection.

But only in the last few years have these differences in worldview exploded into an all-out culture war.

As an investigative reporter, I was given unprecedented insider access to the historic Spot vs. Mittens election, a campaign that ripped, scratched, and nipped our country apart. In these pages, I chronicle this historic contest from the early primaries to the heavily contested results.

I hope that this book satisfies two distinct audiences: political junkies and pet lovers. For political junkies, I offer a Bob Woodward–esque attention to detail, getting deep inside the minds of the fluffy animals who run our country.

For cat and dog lovers, I reveal the intense planning and polling that precedes every one of those cute, goofy things your pet does. You'll never look at them the same way again.

Don Asmussen,
Washington, D.C.

★ PET ★
ELECTIONS
A PRIMER

★ Every four years, the proud people of America (divided into a
   Dog Lovers Party and a Cat Lovers Party—and occasionally a
   third-pet party) gather at the polls to elect the pet they think
   can best protect this country from intruders/pests.

★ Though pet elections have taken place for decades, they've
   only been *officially* recognized since 1960, due mostly to the
   plummeting popularity of our human candidates. In contrast,
   people still trust animals. This book may change this.

★ Pet elections are reported by *Homo sapiens* who work for
   the "pet press" (which includes *Dog Fancy, Cat Fancy, Cat
   World, Dog & Kennel,* the *Bark,* the *Meow, Cat & Dog
   Quarterly,* and various local cat and dog newspapers). All of
   these publications promise that no cat or dog bias affects
   their coverage. Yeah, *right.*

★ THE PLAYERS ★

A GUIDE TO THE IMPORTANT PETS IN THIS BOOK

SPOT

The incumbent, Spot, is a German shepherd. His "War on Squirrels" may hurt his reelection chances.

MITTENS

The Cat Party's timid nominee, Mittens is moody, aloof, and always hard to find (on issues).

KARL ROVER

Also known as "Spot's brain." A Chihuahua, Rover denies accusations that Spot's first-term win was fixed (or spayed).

DICK MORRIS THE CAT

This Cat Party consultant is a turncat (he'll consult for whichever party offers him Sheba). His secret: *a paw fetish*.

VICE PRESIDENT DICK CHEWTOY
A longtime Dog Party operative, Chewtoy pushed for the "War on Squirrels." His ties to Alpo, Inc., raise conflict-of-interest concerns.

ANCHOR WOOF BLITZER
One of a few journalists who is a furry pet. Woof's show is the first place pet candidates go to deny the latest rumor or scandal.

ACTRESS BETTY WHITE
Golden Girls actress and well-known dog lover. She becomes one of the nation's top critics of the "War on Squirrels."

ISHMAEL THE IV (A GOLDFISH)
A surprisingly strong third-party pet candidate. His no-nonsense style may lead to him floating to the top.

POLLY (A NORWEGIAN BLUE PARROT)
Another surprisingly strong independent pet candidate. Polly's political strength is his populist ability to repeat whatever voters say.

JANUARY
★ THE IOWA ★ CAT CAUCUS

The Pug Report, an online news site known for its doggish pursuit of slime, just posted a story claiming that Mittens, the current favorite for the Cat Party nomination, has vomited for the *twelfth time* in two hours. The scoop, unconfirmed, suggests that a witness saw the candidate "obsessively chewing on a plastic bag" as recently as 11:23 p.m. last night (likely explaining the persistent vomiting). Mittens's closest challengers, Patches (a Vermont Manx) and Midnight (the party's first black-cat candidate in its history), are sure to take advantage. Mittens must respond *quickly*, before the mainstream press jumps on it.

A meeting is called. Mittens, loath to reveal his plastic bag addiction, suggests a distraction: a cute photo-op of him lapping milk falling from an Iowa cow's dangling udders. All agree. A cow is booked for 4 p.m. ET. *This is no time for pride.*

The Pug Report posts latest Mittens scandal.

PET ELECTIONS—CAN THE CAT COME BACK?

As I envision Mittens lapping milk from under that cow, I can't help but think back to the book that influenced me and so many other journalists interested in getting into the world of pet punditry. Author Theodore White's eye-opening Purrlitzer Prize–winning book, *The Petting of the President,* 1960, was the first attempt *ever* to cover a pet election in detail. Although dog and cat lovers had long admitted, in secret, that their pets actually ran their lives (and their country), it wasn't until 1960 that a book confirmed it.

1960: J. F. Kittedy wins first televised pet debate when nervous opponent pants before cameras.

White's best-seller followed the campaign of J. F. Kittedy, a sleek, telegenic tabby from Massachusetts. Its contents were a revelation. Today, with a public bludgeoned by forty years of quick-cut, hyperkinetic Meow Mix ads, it's almost impossible to explain the impact of the static image of a handsome J. F. Kittedy purring and batting away questions during the first televised pet debate in 1960. He was *adorable*.

MITTENS AND THE WEIGHT OF PET HISTORY

Alas, Mittens is no J. F. Kittedy. Today, cat lovers do still exist, but most have become disillusioned after years of erratic feline behavior. The Cat Party, now perceived as lazy, finicky, and self-centered, has fallen behind the Dog Party over the last two decades. The constant vomiting, the peeing on rugs, the scratching of new furniture—all have taken their toll. Lap sitting is no longer enough.

Of course, cats have done little to reverse this slide, relying on shallow cuteness for years, always depending on yet another cat calendar or cat poster to sustain party interest. Perhaps the nadir of this disturbing trend was Geraldine Furraro's embarrassing "Hang in There, Baby!" campaign slogan, which served as a perfect metaphor for the Cat Party's growing irrelevance.

MITTENS'S OPPONENT

Today, with Mittens in the classic "Furraro" mold, the closest this contest has to a J. F. Kittedy is Vermont's charismatic and innovative Patches, a Manx. Firstly, *he has no tail*, making him extremely difficult to chase down on any number of issues. He literally has nothing back there to grab on to, except a slight nub. In a long race, having no tail is a *huge* advantage.

Geraldine Furraro's ill-advised "Hang in There, Baby!" poster.

PATCHES, YOUNG VOTERS, AND THE INTERNET

In another link to J. F. Kittedy, Patches makes use of the newest technology to get his message out there. For Kittedy, this was TV. For Patches, it's the Internet. While traditional pet candidates like Mittens choose *Cat Fancy* magazine as their political mouthpiece, Patches posts his image on popular Web sites like Stuff on My Cat and the Infinite Cat Project, reaching millions of potential voters.

THE IOWA COW MILK LAPPING PHOTO OP DEBACLE

With Patches securing the young vote, Mittens focuses on the older cat lovers—hence his "Iowa cow milk lapping photo op" strategy. It nostalgically suggests the '50s, a simpler era when cats still had the time to do adorable things on farms. And it would, hopefully, refocus the attention from Mittens's (rumored) *decadent* addiction to plastic bags to his *wholesome* love of cream.

The cow shoot goes without incident, and the footage is quickly edited for maximum impact and sent out to all the local media outlets. Several stations show it on their 10 p.m. news broadcasts.

Satisfied, an exhausted Mittens retires for the night.

The next morning, a call wakes him up. It is 5 a.m.

"Get in here," an anxious-sounding campaign intern spits.

Negative Register & Democat *reaction to Mittens's "Iowa cow milk lapping" photo op.*

In a huge miscalculation, Mittens had failed to gauge the changing moral climate in Iowa since the Janet Jackson wardrobe malfunction in 2004. "Exposed cow teat fear" grips Iowa. Mittens's numbers dive.

Desperate, he calls Dick Morris the Cat. It's his only option.

POLITICAL ADVISER DICK MORRIS THE CAT

Dick Morris the Cat doesn't *do* subtle. And now, with only two days remaining before the Iowa Cat Caucus, he can't afford to. Mittens, clearly uncomfortable with Morris's secret new strategy, hides under the hotel bed while Morris and I speak.

Dick Morris the Cat (seen here in late 2004).

"I always go back to that old political TV ad "Daisy," Morris tells me, referring to the infamous 1964 TV spot showing a little girl picking petals from a daisy as a voice-over counts down to a nuclear explosion. *Subtle.*

"Only one thing scares voters more than exposed teats, and that's *nuclear war*." Morris claims. "Now, I ask you, what's the main difference between Mittens, an Angora, and Patches, a Manx?"

"A tail," I answer, confused.

"Bingo. My guy, he's *got* a tail. You can read his moods, right? If he were dangerous for the country, his tail would be twitching all wacky and stuff. But it's *not*—he's calm, resolute, steady." Morris continues, "But Patches . . . *no tail*! What's he thinkin'? Who knows! Maybe he's thinkin' about starting a *nuclear war*!" And with this, Morris shows me pictures of his fourteen kittens. And he begins to weep.

THE FIRST TV ATTACK AD

Morris's first TV spot, titled "Manx Stanks," is set to premiere tonight at 6 p.m. (and will repeat all night). I sit to watch it in my hotel room.

"Daisy" TV ad links Patches and nuclear war.

The ad opens, much like the 1964 "Daisy" spot, with a little girl sitting in a field of flowers. She is joined by what appears to be Patches (a look-alike). She happily asks him how many lives he has. The Patches character counts them, starting at nine (an Intelligent Design theory claims that cats have nine lives). Slowly he counts down, "nine . . . eight . . . seven . . . six . . . five. . .," but then his voice turns to a more ominous tone, continuing, "four . . . three . . . two . . ." Suddenly, a blast is heard and a mushroom cloud appears. Then, chilling words slowly fade in across the screen: "Patches may have nine lives . . . but your children don't." In just under thirty seconds, *everybody* in Iowa forgets about Mittens's exposed cow teats. Patches is toast.

The final chilling moments of the "Daisy" ad.

PATCHES PULLS OUT OF THE RACE

Within seconds of the first airing of the "Manx Stanks" TV spot, Patches's team knows he's finished, with Iowans instantly perceiving him as feral and tailless, i.e., morally rudderless. He will pull out.

By 6:10 p.m., Patches is before the cameras. He is weeping. His wife is by his side, along with their twelve kittens.

Patches (with family) announces he's out.

Dick Morris the Cat is watching Patches's announcement on the hotel bar's television. He can't hide his excitement. Patches looks devastated, his whiskers inert. "If he *had* a tail, it would be between his legs right now," exclaims Morris, his voice echoing throughout the nearly empty bar.

On the TV, Patches speaks of simple pleasures in life ("little toy balls with bells in them," "string") as he tries to remain positive. He tells the audience that he'll take some time off at his kitty condo in upper Vermont to lick his wounds (and privates) while he decides what to do next. His followers cheer, and he is gone.

Patches may be finished, but Dick Morris the Cat is not. Not even close. It is now 6:25 p.m., only five minutes since Patches pulled out, but there's still more work to do. Tomorrow is the primary, and *one* other candidate profited from Patches's sudden resignation. That candidate's name is Midnight.

IS AMERICA READY TO ELECT A BLACK CAT?

A bit of pet political history for you: The U.S. has *never* elected a black cat to lead the country. Racism? No. Superstition? Oh, yes. *Deep-rooted* superstition. This is why Midnight's recent popularity is so refreshing. For the first time in pet history, cat lovers are not talking about a feline's color; they are talking about his *ideas*. Not for long.

"Midnight," another Iowa frontrunner.

I hear rumors that Morris has a TV ad ready to take out Midnight. I look for Mittens for a comment. He's hiding. Then I see his tail.

I kneel beside the bed and speak into the darkness underneath, hoping to engage the hidden candidate. Nothing. I make little kissy noises, a tactic that usually draws out even the toughest feline interview subject. Nothing. I use a string. He lunges. Got 'im.

Mittens, speaking from underneath his hotel bed.

I ask him about the new TV ad, ready to broadcast in just a few minutes. I ask him if it plays the cat color card. Shamed silence.

Superstition is a funny thing. Midnight is a quality candidate, willing to talk about *solutions*, but many pet lovers fear he might cross their path. It's *impossible* to campaign across Iowa without crossing a voter's path.

I ask Mittens what he thinks of Midnight. "He's a good kitty," is all he'll offer. I ask him again if they're playing the cat color card. Seeing I'd loosened my grip, Mittens suddenly springs from my arms and back under his hotel bed. There's my answer.

The next day, Mittens wins the primary paws down. A blowout. Midnight gets barely 2 percent of the vote. So much for substance.

Mittens is well on his way to the Cat Party nomination.

I go to his room for a post-win interview.

He is still under the bed.

2

FEBRUARY

★ MEET ★
KARL ROVER

There is nothing like watching Spot run. Ask anyone. He's like a big, furry child, eager to please and just so damn glad to be *outside*. It's no wonder people voted for him.

No logic, no pattern to his choices, just back and forth, back and forth, round and round, as if chasing some invisible squirrel. Adorable, hysterical, crazy . . . *carefully planned* . . . chaos. Carefully planned? Meet political adviser Karl Rover.

Karl Rover helped Spot's first run in 1998.

"Dog people love that enthusiasm, that goofy energy," boasts Rover, who has agreed to sit with me to discuss Spot's long-running Dog Party successes. "That invisible squirrel routine," I ask. "Is it not a visual metaphor for your client's current political situation—the running in circles after an imaginary enemy?"

Rover, looking displeased, abruptly ends the interview.

HITTING A RUFF SPOT

Rover realizes Spot's biggest problem during his first term has been *unplanned* chaos. The last few years have been difficult ones, especially for dogs. Needless to say, leash laws have divided the country. The problem: A *very small* segment of the dog population continues to poop in other people's yards. It's a delicate balancing act for the Dog Party, which preaches *less* government oversight. Predictably, the rival Cat Party calls for *stricter* leash laws.

But the real issue is a certain war Spot started two years ago.

"War on Squirrels" updates on C-SPOT channel.

"WAR ON SQUIRRELS"

Originally sold to American pet lovers as a way to protect the country's numerous bird feeders from scavenging, twitchy-tailed insurgents, Spot's embattled "War on Squirrels" has no end in sight. No matter how many squirrels are caught by our nation's courageous canines, more seem to spring up every day. The situation has gotten so out of control that birds (whose feeders are directly affected and who normally side with dogs on political issues) are rumored to be in negotiations *to give their endorsement to the Cat Party*!

Spot's attempts to calm the public (by licking their faces and fetching their slippers) are no longer working, and predictably, Vice President Dick Chewtoy's daily announcement of an imminent squirrel surrender is making even cats howl. Chaos rules.

On February 8, a meeting of the top Spot team leaders is finally called. Karl Rover runs it. The "War on Squirrels" is starting to affect Spot's popularity numbers, and the loss of the Bird Party's endorsement is a major concern, he says. Dogs need something that will inspire America's dog lovers. What should it be?

C. M. Coolidge's rendering of alleged secret dog meeting to plan the new war.

DOG PARTY: WOULD ANOTHER WAR HELP?

A decision is quickly made that *a second war* is needed to distract from the current unpopular one, and quickly. Vice President Dick Chewtoy suggests a war on *cars* (an age-old dog nemesis).

But a war on cars has inherent problems. It's fine, in photo ops, for Spot to occasionally chase a car. It shows initiative. But no dog has ever *caught* a car in America's long history. How do you sell the country on a war against something that you cannot possibly ever keep up with?

Enter Karl Rover.

"The idea isn't to sell the idea that dogs *can* catch cars. The idea is to sell the idea that cats *can't.*"

Spot speaking to the U.N. about cars.

Justifying the "War on Cars"

Rover is a genius. The downside of a "War on Cars" is fairly obvious: They're impossible to catch. But the upside is two-fold: It marginalizes both cats *and* squirrels, their party's two biggest enemies. Cats, according to Rover, are constantly running away from cars, much too frightened to stay and fight. "They'd rather negotiate, or sleep on top of the enemy," Rover exclaims. "You'll never see a dog sleeping on top of a car. Never!" And squirrels? "Two words: *street pizza*." He goes on, "No squirrel has

CAT PARTY:
SOFT ON CARS

CATNAPPING ON TOP OF THE ENEMY?

Mittens seen sleeping atop a Buick — *that hates our freedom.*

THE PUG REPORT®

"We must bark at them, not sleep on

Mittens: "I was not napping, I was spying."

The Pug Report exploits a Cat Party weakness.

ever survived a fight with an automobile. Just look on any highway. In fact, with our 'War on Cars,' even if a dog *never* catches one car, there's still a good chance that the car he's chasing might hit a squirrel, in turn helping . . . the 'War on Squirrels.'"

As usual, Karl Rover has every angle figured out.

★ AMERICA'S ★
WAR
★ ON CARS ★

THEY HATE OUR FREEDOM

C-SPOT "War on Cars" — Already not going well.

"War on Cars" logo premieres.

Selling a Second War

Only one hurdle remains: Spot needs to convince the nation's dog lovers that cars represent an imminent threat to our nation's dog safety. But how? Rover has a friend at the influential *Bark* magazine, he says. It was time to call in a favor.

Pet magazine and pet newspaper headlines show different takes on the two current wars.

USING THE PET MEDIA TO SELL A WAR

This new "War on Cars" would have to start soon, preferably before the national pet debate in October. Spot is excited to be chasing something new, especially with the political quagmire the "War on Squirrels" has become. And the *pet press* will help!

THE MODERN DOG CULTURE MAGAZINE

THE

BARk

FEBRUARY/MARCH

SHOULD DOGMA
AND STATE MIX?

WEGMAN'S
ELECTION PICKS

LEASH LAWS

COUNTDOWN
ANCHOR KEITH
DOBERMANN IS
A CAT LOVER (!)

SEE SPOT
RUN

DOG HIT BY CAR

The February/March cover of the Bark.

The first story, featured in the *Bark* magazine's February issue, is small, and most readers may not even notice it among the various dog tricks and grooming stories. But it's there, at the bottom right-hand corner: DOG HIT BY CAR.

The details are scant, and the source is unidentified. All that is known is that a seeing-eye dog—*the most selfless of all canines*—had been mowed down by a speeding automobile. According to a witness, the car never stopped. The dog died. What is unusual is that the story is appearing in the *Bark* magazine, which usually focuses on *positive* pet stories. The byline: *Judith Miller*.

ENTER JUDITH MILLER

Reporter Judith Miller was new at the *Bark* magazine, having recently been forced out of the *New York Times* (a newspaper that covers *Homo sapiens*). New to the pet beat, Miller needed a big story. Karl Rover needed some help. It was synergy.

With Miller's hire, the *Bark* editors were pushing their reporters to dig up more hard-hitting fare, mostly in response to the recent emergence of opinionated dog blogs (like the Pug Report, on which dog lovers discuss leash laws, squirrel attacks, and any number of cat-related scandals). Karl Rover's call was a dogsend.

Friends Judith Miller and Karl Rover in 1998.

BUILDUP TO WAR

A follow-up to Miller's DOG HIT BY CAR story, titled ANOTHER DOG HIT BY CAR, is in the very next issue of the *Bark*. In this story, a chilling quote is placed toward the end of its third paragraph. The quote, ". . . cars *hate* our [dogs'] freedom," is the first time any pet publication has suggested that roadkills are a purposeful attack on canine rights. Upping the ante, Miller's next story, the speculative EVEN MORE DOGS WILL BE HIT BY CARS VERY, VERY SOON, suggests that a preemptive strike is imperative, *post haste*. Dog lovers nationwide, overtaken by car fear, call on their canine leadership to become proactive. Karl Rover's plan is working. The country is primed for another war.

SPOT ON TV: "CAR INSPECTIONS HAVE FAILED"

On cue, Spot appears on Woof Blitzer's show, having agreed to announce the start of the war on the C-SPOT channel.

"Car inspections have failed, Woof. Their stalling tactics have fooled us for long enough. Cars *hate* our freedom," Spot repeats.

Surprisingly, Woof Blitzer shoots back a tough question.

"President Spot, I would be remiss not to mention that your Dog Party's position against leash laws, in some way, may have contributed to the amount of dogs being hit by cars. No?" asks

Blitzer. Television viewers are stunned by this hardball query.

Spot takes a moment to think. Behind the cameras, Karl Rover is seething. "Blitzer is a *cat* at heart, always hiding under the bed of idealism," he tells me, his tail whipping. Blitzer had promised not to bring up this contradiction on air. He lied, *like a cat.*

Woof Blitzer puts Spot on the spot.

Fortunately, Rover had prepped Spot just in case this happened. Spot looks straight into the camera, tilts his head just slightly, and gives that quizzical look that dogs do so well.

It is so cuuute!

Spot's approval rating jumps 15 percent after the head tilt. The "War on Cars" wins approval the next day.

3

MARCH

★ HE'S ★
UNDER THE BED

Anyone who has ever owned a cat knows that when confronted with a difficult issue, they will inevitably hide under something (even if it doesn't quite entirely cover them). This is the Cat Party's legacy. And Dick Morris the Cat must change this old perception if felines really want to win this election.

Mittens has remained under his hotel bed for three entire weeks (he was reportedly spooked by a rumor that reporters were going to ask for his opinions on issues). Unable to tempt him back out, all I can see is light occasionally reflecting off his eyes.

Mittens is no J. F. Kittedy, I think. But then, was J. F. Kittedy ever really J. F. Kittedy? Though most cat lovers look back nostalgically to 1960 and the golden J. F. Kittedy era (dubbed "Catelot" by admirers for its glamour and taste—*cat-fish* was served at the White House), a closer look reveals a very different story. It isn't pretty.

The embattled Mittens, still under his hotel bed.

J. F. Kittedy and the Real Legacy of Catelot

As I mentioned earlier, Kittedy exploited the new medium of television to revolutionize pet campaigning as we knew it in 1960. Unfortunately, this new medium valued *image* over *substance*, and, in some ways, the Cat Party has never recovered.

J. F. Kittedy was a Massachusetts cat of privilege, and dog lovers openly questioned a cat's ability to lead the country in time of war. The Cuban Dog Whistle Crisis of 1961 had been a growing concern for America's canines, but the nation's cats dismissed it (mostly due to the fact that only dogs could hear the whistles). But, in an attempt to show dog lovers that a cat *could* protect the country just as well as any dog could, Kittedy secretly plotted an ill-advised invasion.

Fido Castro in Cuba in January 1961.

Failed Overthrow of Fido Castro

With the rise of Communism, America's dogs were on edge. In mid 1961, Kittedy, financing clawed Cuban cat exiles, launched an attempt to overthrow the Cuban government of the feisty Fido Castro, who had built the offending dog whistles (aimed at the United States).

The U.S.-backed coup attempt fell apart when said cats suddenly realized that the attack would entail traveling by water. Predictably, they went missing.

J. F. KITTEDY AND THE BAY OF PUGS

As the public relations disaster unfolded across television screens, U.S. dogs whined. The Bay of Pugs, the cutest thing you will *ever* see (photo below), would remain under the clenched red paw of Communism. J. F. Kittedy never recovered. He spent his last years inviting a succession of lovelies to his bed (well, actually *under* it).

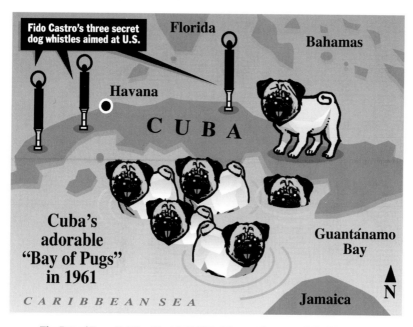

The Bay of Pugs, Pet President J. F. Kittedy's most famous political faux-paw.

CAN MITTENS REINVENT THE CAT PARTY?

Dick Morris the Cat dismisses all Cat Party history. "That was over forty years ago," says Morris, "and I think a lot of dog lovers who are concerned about this never-ending 'War on Squirrels' are looking for an alternative." He doesn't sound convinced.

A sudden, guttural noise comes from beneath the hotel bed. It is Mittens. He is throwing up, again.

I look at Morris. I ask him if a candidate that throws up four-teen times a day can possibly protect the country from intruders.

He pretends he doesn't hear my question.

I ask him again.

Visibly annoyed, Morris suddenly bolts under the bed, joining Mittens. I look underneath. They are both waaay over, in the dark corner. They both hiss, disapprovingly.

I briefly consider using string.

But then I decide to let them be.

4

APRIL

★ DOGMA ★ VS. CATMA

A s everyone knows, Spot believes deeply in *Dog*.
Nearly every decision he makes derives from his relationship with the Heavenly Dog. This includes the "War on Squirrels," which Spot claims Dog suggested to him in a doggie dream.

Karl Rover, not a particularly religious dog himself, respects Spot's beliefs. He's also very aware that Spot's beliefs could help him win reelection. That's why the "Under Dog" trial is perfect.

The Pledge of Obedience is currently under attack by an out-of-the-mainstream feral cat from Barkeley, California. The cat argues that the phrase "Under Dog," which was added to the Pledge in 1952 to battle pinko Communist household mice, is actually *unconstitutional*. Dogs everywhere howl.

To Karl Rover, the issue is a dogsend, whatever you believe in.

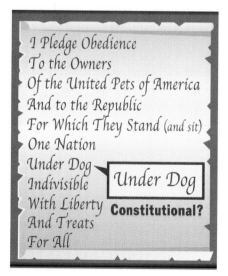

I Pledge Obedience
To the Owners
Of the United Pets of America
And to the Republic
For Which They Stand (and sit)
One Nation
Under Dog
Indivisible
With Liberty
And Treats
For All

Under Dog
Constitutional?

The Pledge of Obedience's "Under Dog".

LET SLIP THE DOGS OF FAITH

Spot's first-term victory was widely attributed to his public relationship with the Heavenly Dog. After years of the Cat Party's dogless celebration of self (perhaps best illustrated by party leader Teddy Kittedy's disgusting habit of bathing himself at hearings), it was a relief knowing Spot would leave his bathing to others.

Teddy Kittedy, J. F. Kittedy's brother, pauses while licking himself during a hearing.

"ONE NATION, UNDER DOG, INDIVISIBLE . . ."

The Barkeley cat behind the lawsuit, named Scat, argues in court that allowing the phrase "Under Dog" in the Pledge of Obedience places "undo stress" upon the nation's cats, who instinctively fear dogs and will be *forced*, by schools, to believe that their creator would want to chase them up a tree.

Dog lovers, predictably, are livid. They believe the Pledge of Obedience's "Under Dog" inclusion is comforting, like the entire country is a litter happily suckling freedom from the country's teats.

With such a chasm, a political showdown is inevitable.

The cat and dog press react to the Barkeley "Under Dog" Pledge of Obedience trial.

Most dogs believe in the Heavenly Dog.

Is Someone Watching Over All Pets?

The Pledge of Obedience battle between cats and dogs is actually part of a much larger debate: Who watches over all of us? Is there a Heavenly Dog?

Obviously, the Cat Party has issues with this concept, as the Barkeley cat Scat has made clear. But although the Cat Party is often accused of atheism, this isn't entirely true, either.

Heavenly Dog vs. Science Diet

While most dogs are religious by nature, most cats tend to believe in science, or more specifically, Science Diet cat food.

The Science Diet theory is this: Throughout our planet's long history, cat food has evolved, *randomly*, from the fatty Purina products of several million years ago to the more healthy morsels of today. But it only improves because the laws of evolution dictate that it should.

Of course, dogs argue that a *higher intelligence* must be pouring it into our bowls.

Cats *laugh* at this thought.

Most cats believe in Science Diet cat food.

"The idea of some giant being pouring food into our bowls is something out of the Middle Ages," suggests several prominent Cat Party Science Dietologists, rather condescendingly.

This may turn into a major wedge issue in this pet election.

RELIGION: WILL MITTENS TAKE A STAND?

As the religion issue grows, Dick Morris the Cat realizes that Mittens will have to weigh in on his beliefs. To spur this on, Morris meets with him under his hotel bed, and they discuss the pros and cons of talking a stand this early in the election. While under there, Morris notices that Mittens has been vomiting even more than usual, each puddle containing the wrinkled remnants of chewed plastic bags. He doesn't say anything, but it worries him.

At Morris's urging, Mittens calls a press conference to add his voice to the Heavenly Dog vs. Science Diet debate. Unfortunately, he insists on speaking from under his bed, way over in the darkest corner, making photos almost impossible.

He then, predictably, takes *both* sides of the issue.

SEATTLE SCRATCH POST INTELLIGENCER

"Print" Cloudy, w temperatu in the 80s

VOL. CLV. NO. 52,876   THURSDAY, MARCH 17 $1.00

MITTENS'S POSITION ON 'UNDER DOG?': UNDER BED.

SPOT: VISION TO DEFEAT CARS AND SQUIRRELS CAME TO ME IN DOGGIE DREAM

Spot's divine guidance

Staff Reports

WASHINGTON — While Spot has been outspoken about his faith, Mittens has remained on — no, make that *under*, the fence. At a press conference today, he

Staff Reports

Press reaction to Mittens's under-the-bed press conference is decidedly negative.

The press reaction to Mittens's fence prancing on the theology issue is decidedly negative. To take *all* sides seems gutless, especially when hiding under a bed while doing it.

Spot appears on The O'Rottweiler Factor.

SPOT: ON THE ATTACK

Seeing a perfect moment to slam his November opponent, Spot sits in with Bill O'Rottweiler to discuss his religious beliefs. It is well known that Spot was "Barked Again" over ten years ago, a experience he says saved him from a licking problem which was, in his own words, "destroying my life."

SPOT'S RELATIONSHIP WITH THE HEAVENLY DOG

Those dark days are long over. (Spot discusses them in detail in our official campaign interview, included here in chapter 5.) He tells Bill O'Rottweiler that he's actually praying for Mittens and his rumored plastic bag chewing addiction (a sweet gesture . . . or a chance to mention an opponent's major weakness while on the air?).

In the interview's final seconds, Spot and Bill hold paws and ask the audience to pray along with them for Mittens. It is . . . *brutal.* And it was all Karl Rover's idea.

C-SPOT Election Poll

These numbers are as of April 21.

Do you think a pet candidate that vomits twenty-three times a day can protect the country from squirrels and cars?

88% NO — 10% Yes — 2% Maybe

Mittens's numbers get hurt by the rumors.

WILL MITTENS RESPOND TO SPOT'S ATTACK?

The Spot and Bill O'Rottweiler "praying for Mittens" moment is a major embarrassment to the Cat Party. Mittens needs to get out from under his hotel room bed and show the country that he is fine, that the vomiting rumors on the Internet are not true. Bill Morris the Cat attempts to coax him, but Mittens still resists. He isn't ready.

With his candidate in hiding, Morris has little choice but to go on TV himself. But what issue is a Cat Party strength?

MORRIS: HIT 'EM WHERE IT HURTS

Perhaps the Dog Party's stepped-up attacks on Mittens are to distract from their own failures. Now going on two months, the "War on Cars," has caught *no* cars (to be fair, one *was* questioned and released). What's more, *no* squirrels have been hurt in car-chasing-related accidents. *This is our issue*, Morris realizes. He is ready.

That night, he agrees to appear on Woof Blitzer's show to talk about the many rumors surrounding Mittens's campaign.

The minute the show starts, Morris is on the offensive. He begins by stating that *all* cats, not just Mittens, *should* be hiding under their beds for fear of all the cars still out there on the road. He then proceeds to show shocking photos of roadkill that Spot's administration has prevented pet newspapers from printing. It's chilling.

Dick Morris the Cat shows shocking photos of roadkill that Spot's administration has surpressed.

Watching Morris's performance on Blitzer's show, Karl Rover is angered, but also *impressed*.

Not only has Morris switched the focus back to the war, but he's shifted it completely away from religion, a Dog Party strength.

And all this with a candidate who won't even come out from under a bed.

Karl Rover needs more pets like this on his team.

He files away this thought for later.

5

MAY

★ THE ★
SPOT INTERVIEW

The following two chapters contain one-on-one interviews that I conducted with the two main candidates, Spot and Mittens. Each interview originally appeared within the pages of Cat & Dog Quarterly. *They have been edited for space.*

Q. **Mr. President, do you think you've been a good dog?**

A. Oh yes, I've been a very good dog. Just look at the progress we've made in the "War on Squirrels."

What progress are you referring to?

Well, you wouldn't know it from *Cat Fancy*, but I speak with dogs who are out there in those backyards barking away, and they say the squirrels are losing.

Your critics say "Operation Infinite Barking" accomplishes nothing.

By critics, you mean the cats? [Pause.] They recommend . . . *purring*?

Some Cat Party leaders believe that your administration has pumped up the threat that squirrels pose to our backyards. How do you respond to this?
Anyone who has ever been in a backyard and has seen a squirrel firsthand knows what a threat they are. Birds have told me stories that would make your tail curl, unless you're a Manx. When squirrels die in war, they believe there're seventy-two acorns waiting up in heaven for them. You see? They *want* to die. They *love* acorns!

Fair enough. But why start the "War on Cars" when we're not even close to the end of the "War on Squirrels?"
The "War on Squirrels" is almost finished. There're only *two* left.

Two? There're only two squirrels left? In the country? That can't be right. I just saw four or more on my way here.
Those were probably chipmunks, or badgers. They couldn't have been squirrels, unless you saw only *two* of them, maybe standing next to two badgers. That's possible. Where'd you see 'em?

Let's move on. The "War on Cars," how is that going?
Very well. There're only two cars left. We're winning.

Author Don Asmussen telling Spot to "sit" for his interview.

Mr. President, I just saw a number of cars on the highway.
What number? I'll bet it's *two*!

LEASH LAWS
As you know, the country is divided over leash laws. What's your stance?
I say let the free market determine how much regulation dogs need outside. I don't think the government should be telling dogs what to do.

Critics argue that the panel you put together last year to review the leash law was completely made up of dogs.

That's completely ridiculous.

Your vice president, Dick Chewtoy, still refuses to release the names of the pets who participated on that leash law panel.

They're confidential. If their names were released, special interests would try to influence their decisions. This way, they're safe to make their decisions in the public's best interest.

A list of seven names on that panel was leaked to the popular Internet site Wonkatt. The names were as follows: Fido, Rex, Spike, Trooper, Sparky, Tuffy . . . and Cujo. Those all sound like dog names.

I would have to disagree with you there. I think you're jumping to conclusions. Fido—I'll give you that one. But the others, that's all pure speculation. One was a turtle, I believe.

Fair enough. On that same subject—why is the Dog Party against leash laws, but _for_ cat harnesses? That seems self-serving.

Self-serving? Hardly. It's about city budgeting. Do you know how much it costs every time a fireman has to go rescue someone's cat out of a tree? If all cats had harnesses, those firemen would be free to save people from disasters, terrorists, squirrels, etc. Are you suggesting that all those people who could've been saved now have to die because cats don't want to wear harnesses? That's the very _definition_ of self-serving. That's what you'll get if you elect a cat.

MITTENS, THE OPPONENT

Your opponent, Mittens—what are your thoughts?

[Pause.] Good kitty. Worthy opponent. But . . . does a cat protect a home? I don't know. It's seems to me that cats nap too much. I think now, after 9/11, you need to have a dog near the front door.

A cat is good company for the elderly.
But what if a squirrel gets in? A cat
would *not* protect an elderly person
from a squirrel. Unless, of course,
the squirrel was trying to attack the
elderly person's lap. Then, at least, the
cat would be in the way of the attack,

Mittens, Spot's opponent.

but probably not intentionally. That's the Cat Party slogan, "We'll
Protect Your Laps." [Laughter.]

**Mittens has accused you and your party of running around in circles after an
imaginary enemy.**
Literally or metaphorically?

*1980 delegates cheer for
citizen Spike.*

Both.
Literally, yes. It's fun to run in circles! If
cats weren't sleeping on elderly people's
laps all the time, they'd understand. Now,
metaphorically, no, we are not running in
circles. And squirrels are not imaginary.
They're everywhere, and they *hate* us.

**They're everywhere? I thought you just said
there were only two squirrels left?**
Well, I meant that metaphorically. Literally, the squirrels are here
and there. Two of them. And they're *losing*.

Spot's Father, Spike
Your father, Spike, is a former president. Do you often seek his advice?
My father is a legend. His "War on Mailmen" brought the country
together against an enemy that kept coming back at us every day
around the same time. He never gave up barking. He even dated

one of the Lassies. His image is still used on Alpo cans. I'd be happy to be half of what he is. But do I ask him for advice? No. I look to a higher source for that, the Heavenly Dog. As pilot-author Robert L. Scotty wrote: "Dog is my copilot."

SPOT'S FAVORITE BOOK

You mention author Robert L. Scotty, the Scottish terrier who wrote *Dog Is My Copilot*, a propaganda book published during the six-year "War on Mailmen." Was this book a big influence?

Oh, yeah! I know a lot of today's PC crowd hate all the mailmen bashing in that book, but it's a product of its time. And remember, if the mailmen had won that war, we'd live in a much different world today. But anyway, Scotty's relationship with Dog in

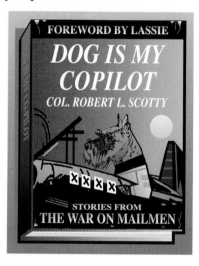

Robert L. Scotty's 1982 book, Dog Is My Copilot.

that book stayed with me. And years later, when I developed a licking problem, I drew a lot of strength from those stories.

Can you describe what your "lost" years were like?

Well, you don't *suddenly* have a licking problem. It develops over a number of years. I was what you call a *functioning licker*. When I was young, I'd have a few licks now and then. It boosted my confidence, took the edge off. But then, suddenly you're seven (forty-two) and you're licking yourself in front of a whole group of people.

So you knew you had a problem.

Of course. But I still wasn't looking for help. That didn't happen until after the car accident.

You were driving? But you're a dog.

Exactly. But on top of that, I was *licking myself* while driving. That's a dangerous combination. Ended up hitting a tree. And then, of course, I peed on the tree, too. I couldn't help myself. I was out of control. My wife, Gretchen, almost left me.

J. F. Kittedy's younger brother, Teddy Kittedy, had an accident around this same time, the Cattaquittic incident.

Good memory, Don. Of course, Teddy fled that scene, as cats do. I stayed at mine. It was a tree, my *territory*. The police showed up, and I was held until my father, Spike, finally bailed me out, like three days later. So I was in the pound for a little bit. Gave me time to think about my life. And then this fellow inmate, named Scrappy, approached me, and asked me if I had a relationship with Dog.

Scrappy-Doo?

Scrappy-Don't, Scrappy-Doo's bad brother. The one you never hear about. He's in for life, but he'd found Dog and this brought him some peace. For the three nights I was in the pound, he taught me *the way*. By the time my father bailed me out, I was a different dog.

THE DOG PARTY'S "PLUTO"-CRATS

There's a lot of concern that your vice president, Dick Chewtoy, was a top dog at Alpo, which was awarded the $30 billion contract to feed our dogs during the recent "War on Cars" and "War on Squirrels."

Absolutely no connection. You been reading *Cat Fancy* again? [Sighs.] Like the Cat Party isn't totally funded by Science Diet! Many of their celebrity cats are Science Dietologists!

Alpo Industries and CEO Pluto the Dog.

Yes, but Science Dietology is a cat religion. Your relationship with Alpo is a business relationship. That's different.

Alpo is more like a religion than you think. It's been with us, like, forever! Did you know "Alpo" is Latin, which is our planet's oldest language? It means "consequently."

That's "ergo," not "Alpo."

I don't think so.

I took Latin in college. "Alpo" is not Latin.

Okay. I think you're confused, but I'll let you have that one. Anyway, my point is that cat religion is the *love of self*. They lick themselves *all* the time. And when I was lost, before that accident, I licked myself all the time, too. So I understand them. That's a very dark place, where we lick ourselves.

FAMILY VALUES

Your wife, Gretchen, says you love Frisbee. That's how you met, right?

Yes, at the dog park! She is the most beautiful corded poodle I have ever laid my nose on. Woof.

Being a female, what does she think of your anti-spaying position?

We have twenty-four puppies, all healthy, thank Dog. She comes from the same place I do. The Cat Party calls it "fixing" — that shows you what they think of family. Spaying, which isn't *fixing* anything, is not in Dog's plan. I see all these spayed pets out there, frolicking in the park.

Spot and his beautiful wife, Gretchen.

When they get up to eight years old (fifty-six), I think they feel empty, lost. I think they wish they hadn't been spayed when they were younger.

So you think the Cat Party's pro-spaying stance is selfish?
Oh, yeah. No one is thinking of the unborn litters. And the Cat Party, their influence is so subtle. Their environmental programs, for an example, their NO LITTERING signs in the dog parks . . . you don't think that subliminally makes young dogs want to get spayed?

I think those signs are about throwing garbage on the ground.
I don't think so.

Well, is there anything we haven't touched upon that you'd like to say something about before we finish here?
Only one thing. I ask dog and cat lovers alike to be patient regarding the "War on Squirrels" and the "War on Cars." We're making a lot of progress on both. I see a day when dogs can walk in backyards and on streets with no fear, no need to bark or run. And I ask all of you, can a cat make this happen? Think about it. I think we *all* know the answer to that.

6

JUNE

★ THE ★
MITTENS INTERVIEW

---

*Getting Mittens to agree to an interview was difficult
and took months to negotiate. Two criteria were demanded:
I could not ask about past sex scandals, and the interview had
to take place under his bed, way over in the corner.*

Q. **Your opponent, Spot, says cats can't defend the country.**

A. Oh, like his wars have made us any safer.
Wouldn't you feel safer with me? Admit it.

Well, yeah, because we're way under a bed.
Exactly. And that would be the Cat Party's war strategy. The
enemy can't possibly reach us back here. Not gonna happen!

**So the Cat Party is recommending that we hide under a bed when an enemy
attacks us?**
No, not just under a bed, but *way in the corner*. That's important.

But can't the enemy just follow you under here?

They can't. Vacuum cleaners have tried, believe me. The space is too tight. We'd *totally* win.

The Cuban revolutionary, Ernesto "Che" Guevara de la Serna, once said, "I'd rather die standing up, than to live on my knees." What would the Cat Party motto be?

Maybe "I'd rather live crouched under here than die crouched out there." [Pause.] How is *this* not winning? We're not dead, and *they can't see us*! [Pause.] I don't understand your point.

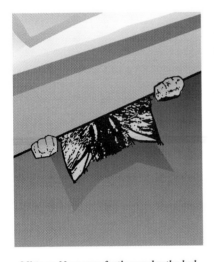

Mittens: Now even further under the bed.

I spoke to Spot about religion, which is shaping up to be a real divisive issue in this upcoming election. What are your beliefs?

What does Spot believe in?

He believes the Heavenly Dog created the yard about three thousand years ago.

How does he explain all the bones found by archeologists?

He believes the Heavenly Dog buried them in the yard. You're a Science Dietologist. How has that changed you?

It's brought me out a bit. I used to hide in the closet. Now I hide under the bed.

Your membership in the Church of Science Dietology has caused some controversy in the dog states. Do you not believe in Dog?

I respect all beliefs. Science Dietology appeals to me, and many cats, because there's no baptism. It's simple: Cats hate water!

Why do you think the Cat Party has lost so much ground to the Dog Party over the last decade?

They play catch, we don't. Their "Man's Best Friend" slogan definitely hurt us.

"Man's Best Friend" was a slogan used for Spot's father Spike's campaign back in 1980. The Cat Party has never been able to better it. Jimmy Catter's 1980 "I'm a Lap President" was as catchy as they come, but it hardly galvanized the base.

Catter's pathetic "I'm a Lap President."

The Dog Party has always defined itself by *what it's against*: They're against mailmen, they're against squirrels, they're against cars, blah, blah blah. Cats aren't as easy to define. T. S. Eliot was right. We're a mystery. And dogs, well, no mystery there. They like food 'n' Frisbee, the two F's. Predictable. Boring. Dumb.

So how will the Cat Party turn things around?

We have to look beyond the laps. Lap sitting is no longer enough. We have to do things we're good at, like mice. People don't realize how many mouse attacks we've prevented. Why hasn't there been a mouse attack in years? Because we prevented it!

You mean all those dead mice you've left at our doors?

Yes! Many of those mice were *number two* in their organization! *High-ranking* mice. But most cat people think, "Oh, he left a gift for us." No, *not* a gift. We just protected your way of life!

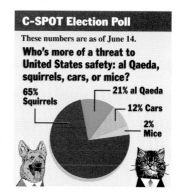

Squirrels or mice? Who's the real threat?

Yet the Dog Party is known as the national security party.
That's the problem our party faces. Cats have to convince American pet lovers that it's not *barking at squirrels* that's making our country safer, it's selective mouse catching.

A suspected number two in the mouse terrorist network, left by the door by Mittens.

On the Plastic Bag Chewing Addiction

I have to ask you about your rumored plastic bag addiction. The online news site the Pug Report has been really riding this story. So, are you really throwing up twenty-three times a day?
Absolutely ridiculous. First of all, why would a cat chew on plastic? That's crazy! If I threw up half as much as the Pug Report says I do, I wouldn't have any time to campaign.

But you haven't been campaigning. You've been under this bed for months.
I'm looking for mice! If we suddenly got attacked by mice, you'd ask me why I *wasn't* under this bed all this time. You reporters are all the same!

They also reported you eat tinsel off Christmas trees and it travels all the way through your system and then out of your butt. True?
I won't dignify that.

So that's not true?

I didn't say it wasn't true. I just said I wouldn't dignify it.

Why chew on Christmas tree tinsel? Isn't it bad for you?

At this moment, Dick Morris the Cat joins us under the bed to discuss a pressing issue with Mittens. They speak in hushed tones for several minutes, and then Morris exits.

LOOK OUT WHEN YOU STEP OUT OF BED, VOTERS!

MITTENS VOMITS ON YOUR SIDE AGAIN

Victim: "It felt really squishy . . . moist . . . I wanted to . . . *die.*"

THE PUG REPORT®

Spot's promise: "I will always make sure to eat my vomit."

Mittens: "It wasn't me."

The Pug Report continues to plague Mittens.

Unearthed 1997 photo of chewed Christmas tree tinsel exiting Mittens's buttocks, posted online.

What was that about?

The Pug Report has *pictures* of the Christmas tree tinsel incident. We have to respond quickly before it snowballs. Morris suggests we spin it so it shows that I support religious holidays. It might bring us some conservative votes. Maybe.

SUCKING THE BREATH OUT OF CHILDREN

Pressing the flesh and kissing babies—they say you cannot win an election without doing a lot of both. How does a cat candidate deal with the irrational Midwestern fear that you might suck out their baby's breath?

Well, that was started by the Dog Party back in 1960, when they knew J. F. Kittedy was gonna win. It was a desperate ploy, using

1960: Midwest newspaper pumps up fear of baby breath–sucking at J. F. Kittedy's expense.

fear. You have to remember, Russia had just launched the *Muttnik 1* satellite.

Muttnik 1 was, of course, the first dog satellite, put in orbit by Soviet canines. It was the height of the Cold War, and U.S. dogs were very paranoid that Russian black terriers had beaten them.

Exactly. That was 1957, so the Cat Party really pushed to reform science (diet) education, to catch us up with the Russians. By 1960, J. F. Kittedy is president, and he wants a cat on the moon!

This all caught the Dog Party by surprise. Remember, their ancestors were the first to howl at the moon, not ours, so they were embarrassed. Space was *their* thing.

So the world is changing fast, and the country is dividing into *pets for science* and *pets for tradition*. Suddenly, fake stories start popping up about cats sucking the breath out of babies in Cincinnati! Talk about the Dark Ages!

So the stories were planted by the Dog Party?

Duh! They were exploiting the Red scare to get votes. Some stories even suggested

October 4, 1957: Black Russian Terriers' Muttnik 1, *first dog satellite, beating the United States to space.*

that cats sucked the breath out of U.S. babies to weaken our future troop numbers against the Soviet Union. It was classic McCattyism.

1960: "McCattyism" was all the rage in newspapers.

In reaction to the baby breath stories, J. F. Kittedy steps right into that stupid Bay of Pugs fiasco, trying to show that he's tough on Commies. We all know how that turned out.

So ironically, those fake baby's breath rumors led to J. F. Kittedy's downfall.

FEAR OF A CATASTROPHIC EVENT

But now, forty years later, some voters still believe that cats suck out the breath of children . . .

Blame 9/11. Pet owners will believe *anything* now. The Dog Party really plays up the "We Protect Your Home" motto. Russian black terriers eventually fell out of power, but now Afghan hounds hate us. When pet owners think protection, they think dogs, not cats.

Again, maybe that's because cats always hide under beds. Look, that's where you are right now.

Okay, I'll give you that. I confess cats haven't exactly helped themselves on this issue. But dogs act like they can stop anything. Let me tell you, Lhasa Apsos have no plan if someone gets in your house. It's all bark.

The Terror Color Codes as seen by people.

The Terror Color Codes as seen by our color-blind canine leaders.

THE LIE OF THE TERROR COLOR CODE

You have been a huge critic of the Terror Color Code Alert System.

Well, yes. It's useless.

Because its constant elevated level has basically just numbed out the general public?

No, no, no. The problem is this: *Dogs can't see colors!* Ask a dog right now what level we're at. You see, it's all black and white to them. And they're protecting us?!

Are cats any better?

Well, we at least see within the spectrum of blues and yellows! That covers "Guarded Condition" and "Elevated Condition," you know. Dogs, they only see black and white, and I'm not talking metaphorically. They look at the Terror Alert System and to them green, blue, and red look the same. Is that who's protecting us? Maybe it's time for the nation's pet owners to see how safe it is here, under this bed. Is the Dog Party's way working? I don't think so.

7

JULY

★ THE ★
WHITE HOUSE LEAK
(ON THE CARPET)

The first that anyone hears of the leak is on the afternoon of July 4. A Woof Blitzer intern receives a mysterious call from an unidentified cat around 2:40 p.m., and it being a holiday, Woof is relaxing atop his kitty condo in nearby Baltimore, Maryland.

According to the source, a dog "far up in the White House" had leaked on the Oval Office carpet over the last two weeks.

This was a huge story.

The intern calls Woof, who is in within the hour. A quick courtesy call is made to the White House to give them a heads-up that the story will be the focus of Woof's show that night. They yalp. The White House pleads to Woof to hold the story. They insist.

Blitzer can't hold the story. He realizes *Cat Fancy* magazine and others

LEAK
★ ON THE ★
WHITE HOUSE
CARPET

WOOF

WOOF!

C-SPOT Identity of White House carpet leaker unknown.

Woof Blitzer breaks the White House leak story.

would accuse his network of helping the Dog Party. He tells the White House the story is running at 6 p.m. ET.

At 5 p.m., Karl Rover calls an emergency meeting of all the top dogs in the administration. Until now, this had been an incredibly tight ship, going on four years with *not one dog ever leaking inside the building.* But recently, things had gotten a little slack, with all the pressure from the two questionable wars making everyone sloppy and less disciplined.

IS NATURE'S MIRACLE ENOUGH?

Woof Blitzer's broadcast sends shockwaves across the country. If dog leadership can't behave themselves, then how can we expect *any* dogs to? This was about *behaving indoors.*

Rover releases a statement to the entire media immediately, stating that White House officials have sprayed "a sizable amount" of Nature's Miracle on the specific area of the Oval Office carpet that was leaked upon, almost entirely ensuring that it would not happen again. Was this enough?

Spot, visibly shaken, meets with Karl Rover. He asks him if he was behind (or over) the leak. Rover says no, he had been let out only minutes before and had "done his business" near the big oak tree near the West Wing. Spot breathed a sigh of relief. He couldn't lose Rover.

But the question remains, who peed in the White House?

Spot tries to cover up White House leak.

VICE PRESIDENT DICK CHEWTOY?

There are two reasons a dog will leak on a carpet: He didn't have access to the outdoors, or he is ill. Seeing that the White House has interns stationed at every exit to allow any prospective leaker easy access to the outdoors, the latter is more likely. So the perpetrator is probably not feeling very well.

The press speculates. Dick Chewtoy has recently had surgery, they figure. Could it be him? Spot and Chewtoy's relationship has been strained since the launch of the "War on Cars" (still no cars caught as of July 5), and he is hesitant to ask his VP directly if he had piddled on the Oval Office carpet.

And Chewtoy himself isn't offering any clues, as usual.

The embattled Vice President Dick Chewtoy.

FINNISH SPITZGERALD NAMED TO LEAD LEAK INVESTIGATION

With pressure mounting to calm a weary public over the indoor behavior of the Dog Party, Spot appoints Finnish Spitzgerald to lead the investigation into the source of the leak. Known as a "bark pointer," his breed indicates the position of his game within ten months or less.

Upon his appointment, Finnish Spitzgerald's first move greatly alarms the Dog Party—he subpoenas Scooby-Doo Libby, who is Dick Chewtoy's assistant. This is not good. There isn't enough Nature's Miracle in the world to get rid of this odor, Spot reasons. How can we sweep this under the rug, when it's *in* the rug?

WILL THE CAT PARTY GET A LEG UP?

The Dog Party leak scandal seems like an early Christmas gift to the Cat Party. But some cat lovers wonder if the timid felines will take advantage of it or just remain in hiding.

Dick Morris the Cat is ecstatic. Finally, a scandal that could distract from Mittens's vomiting problem. Urine definitely trumps vomit, he figures. Now, if only he could get Mittens to agree to come out from underneath that hotel bed to fight back!

An old flame, Gennipurr Flowers, tells on Mittens.

A new slogan, "Mittens: On the Sand, Not in the Papers" is targeted directly at conservative dog lovers so offended by the leak coverage that they might jump over to the cleaner Cat Party.

"I'M GENNIPURR FLOWERS"

Unfortunately, before the paint is even dry on his new campaign posters, Mittens's past catches up with him.

Only one day after the Dog Party leak story breaks, a rather fluffy-looking Ragdoll cat named Gennipurr Flowers calls a press conference. The salivating Pug Report will be blogging it live.

"I am Gennipurr Flowers," says the teary-eyed fluff ball. "And I had a one-year affair with Mittens, the Cat Party's candidate for president." The entire press corps gasps.

Gennipurr Flowers on the cover of the June Fluffy Tail, *which documents their affair.*

So much has been made of Mittens's plastic chewing obsession and vomiting that few had remembered his other addiction: mating. Gennipurr Flowers quickly reminds everyone.

Why now? The timing seems odd, coming only one day after the Dog Party's leak scandal. Are the dogs secretly financing her? *Fluffy Tail*, a seedy fur magazine known for getting celebrity cats to show their stomachs, is sponsoring her press conference. She has posed for their June issue, and her descriptions of her affair with Mittens accompany her pictures. It's on the stands within a week.

DUELING DENIALS

Both Mittens and Vice President Dick Chewtoy issue simultaneous denials for their prospective scandals. A weary public takes them with a grain of salt. Pet owners know the drill. Animals always deny, but their body language betrays them. Just look at them—Chewtoy is slouching and turning to run as he reads his denial. And, revealingly, Mittens reads his from under his bed.

While Mittens hides, Gennipurr Flowers tells the press a lurid tale that would arch any cat's back. Mating, biting, Sheba, mating, more Sheba, biting, Sheba, more mating, etc. Eeew. Hearing it makes you want to clean yourself for a week. Of course, it's *his* word against *yours*, the press tells Flowers. No, I have a tape recording, she purrs. Total silence. What did she just say?

"I have a tape recording," Gennipurr says, again.

She plays a small section of the tape for the press. The recording is of a rendezvous Mittens and she had in his estate's backyard last September. It kept many neighbors awake. Transcript below.

With recorded proof, this will be a hard scandal to wiggle out of. Dick Morris the Cat will need more than Nature's Miracle.

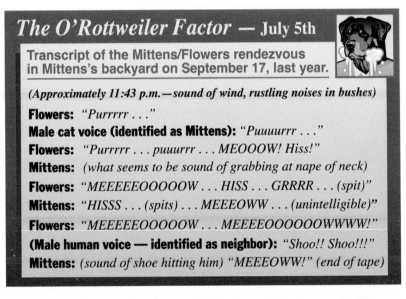

The O'Rottweiler Factor — July 5th

Transcript of the Mittens/Flowers rendezvous in Mittens's backyard on September 17, last year.

(Approximately 11:43 p.m. — sound of wind, rustling noises in bushes)

Flowers: *"Purrrrr . . ."*
Male cat voice (identified as Mittens): *"Puuuurrr . . ."*
Flowers: *"Purrrrr . . . puuurrr . . . MEOOOW! Hiss!"*
Mittens: *(what seems to be sound of grabbing at nape of neck)*
Flowers: *"MEEEEEOOOOOW . . . HISS . . . GRRRR . . . (spit)"*
Mittens: *"HISSS . . . (spits) . . . MEEEOWW . . . (unintelligible)"*
Flowers: *"MEEEEEOOOOOW . . . MEEEEOOOOOOWWWW!"*
(Male human voice — identified as neighbor): *"Shoo!! Shoo!!!"*
Mittens: *(sound of shoe hitting him)* *"MEEEOWW!"* *(end of tape)*

The O'Rottweiler Factor *plays the tape of Flowers's recorded rendezvous with Mittens.*

VP DICK CHEWTOY HAS MORE SURGERY

Perhaps to distract from their own scandal, the White House announces that Chewtoy has had another successful, but unspecified, surgery.

CATS USA EXCLUSIVE: GENNIPURR FLOWERS STILL LOVES MITTENS

SPOT: "I'M A GOOD BOY"

CATS USA

JULY SPECIAL ELECTION E...

"WE ARE ADDICTED TO YARN"

DEMOCAT & CHRONICLE

VOL. CLV. NO. 51,234   MONDAY, JULY 22 $1.00

MITTENS'S INTERN ALSO TELLS OF AFFAIR

'I NEVER WASHED THE BLUE DRESS HE VOMITED ON,' ADMITS MONICAT MEV...

JULY ISSUE

OUTSIDE THE BOX

FOR ANIMALS WHO THINK THEY'RE *HOMO SAPIENS*

"AT SOME POINT, EVERY ANIMAL THINKS IT'S A HOMO SAPIENS."
— Mittens

MITTENS ON DICK CHEWTOY'S DAUGHTER, SCIENCE DIETOLOGY, AND WHY THE MICE ARE WINNING.

Page 22

the furball stain.

FURBALL DNA

THE LEAK: ANOTHER WATERBOWLGATE?

DAILY WOOFER

'DOG WHISPERER' CESAR MILLAN:

'YOU'VE GOT TO RUB HIS NOSE IN IT'

'CHEWTOY WILL JUST LEAK AGAIN IF HE'S NOT PUNISHED'

STAFF REPORTS

WASHINGTON — Dog trainer Cesar Millan says a firm *"Tsssst!"* at Chewtoy every time he leaks should remind him who's boss. (See page 12)

Entert... July 12

"It was a quid pro lhasa apso relationship"

Press reaction roundup on the dueling Dog and Cat Party scandals.

Chewtoy in Washington sporting a head cone

Chewtoy's operation, like Gennipurr Flowers's press conference, is perfectly timed. With federal investigator Finnish Spitzgerald on his tail, Chewtoy's recovery affords him an excuse to avoid undue stress. Respectfully, Spitzgerald gives Chewtoy some time, but only temporarily.

Meanwhile, Washington veterinarians fashion a cone for Chewtoy to wear around his head, in order to keep him from chewing at his own stitches. A normal precautionary move, claim White House officials.

That cone will come to be an important symbol of the party's attitude come November.

MORE MITTENS SCANDAL

As if Flowers wasn't enough, another of Mittens's former maters talks to the press. Monicat Mewinsky, an intern, reportedly had an affair with Mittens two years ago. And like Flowers, she has evidence: She never washed the blue dress he threw up on during one of their secret encounters. When it rains, it purrs.

8

AUGUST

★ THE THIRD-PARTY ★ PET CANDIDATES

With the disturbing Cat and Dog Party scandals of the last few weeks souring the country, the weaknesses of our two-pet-party system are exposed for all to see. With cats heavily funded and controlled by Science Diet Cat Food, Inc., and dogs beholden to Alpo's "Pluto"-crats, the nation's pet owners are starting to realize that their animals have little interest in their needs.

In this vacuum, a new kind of pet candidate often emerges.

Ishmael the IV, a goldfish pet candidate.

"CALL ME ISHMAEL"

Goldfish have always been the kind of pet that people purchase when they don't want the hassles that come with larger animals.

So it's no surprise when a little-known third-party fish from Delaware, Ishmael the IV, finds his numbers suddenly edging upward as the nation's pet lovers grow weary of cats and dogs.

A History of Third-Party Pet Candidates

Ishmael the IV's timing is perfect. While numerous third-party pets have participated in past elections, none have ever received more than the 78,127 votes Godzilla (an iguana), got when he ran for the Green Party back in 1984 (that unusually high total may

have been due to the abysmal, and already critiqued, "Hang in There, Baby" campaign run by the Cat Party's nominee Geraldine Furraro).

Third-party pets are often unusual: Any kind of lizard, exotic bird, alpaca, and even a small rock back in 1976 *(see left)*, will fit the bill. But their high *novelty* factor usually results in early leads and extremely sudden, precipitous drops.

Past third-party pet candidates
(i.e. Unusual Pet Syndrome).

Can a Goldfish Lead Our Country?

Ishmael the IV, being a goldfish, is a bit more mainstream than a lizard, alpaca, or small, heavily marketed rock. He could appeal to traditional pet owners (who hasn't owned a fish?) *and* younger pet owners (sick of the traditional dogs and cats). Ishmael's other upside: If voters tire of him, his life expectancy is *very* short.

How short? If his water isn't changed every week, he could be dead in . . . well, a week. With the thought of another four years of Spot (or four years of looking for Mittens under beds), a week of Ishmael isn't really that unappealing to voters.

His campaign exploits this—his slogan, "Four More Weeks," instead of the classic "Four More Years," assures the nation's pet lovers that he won't be around long enough to hate.

Third-party candidate Ishmael's slogans.   *Florida's Polly the Parrot enters the race.*

POLLY WANTS A CRACK AT IT

As Ishmael's numbers rise, another third-party candidate starts ruffling his feathers in Florida. Polly, a Norwegian Blue parrot, has gotten fawning press due to his innate ability to mimic even the most outrageous campaign promises. Repeating *everything* that the attention-starved voters ask (the only known pet to do this), he is mining the populist vote effectively. He is one to watch.

"War on Squirrels" and "War on Cars" protests help fuel interest in Ishmael and Polly.

With the growing unpopularity of Spot's two wars and Mittens's near void as a Cat Party leader, both of the these two new candidates may have a better chance than in years past. Though birds are messy and extremely loud, voters may forgive this if Polly promises to bring the dogs back home. And as a goldfish, Ishmael has plenty of experience in the fishbowl-type existence that typifies living in the White House. Emboldened by his latest numbers, the cocky goldfish schedules a press conference in Texas, a Dog Party stronghold.

TRAGEDY STRIKES

Minutes before he's scheduled to speak, staffers find Ishmael floating at the top of his bowl.

Ishmael the IV is *dead*.

Before all momentum is lost, another goldfish is purchased and quickly named Ishmael the V.

His numbers remain steady.

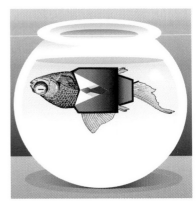

Ishmael the IV's untimely death.

DOG LEAK INVESTIGATION SPREADS

Despite the new problem of more challengers entering the race, Karl Rover and Spot have more pressing concerns. White House–appointed investigator Finnish Spitzgerald has forced a frightened Scooby-Doo Libby to *connect* Vice President Dick Chewtoy to the leak found on the Oval Office rug. Plus, DNA test results are imminent. Spot has yet to directly ask Chewtoy whether the leak came from him. Maybe this is the time.

On the afternoon of August 6, Spot and Dick Chewtoy finally sit down to discuss the situation. After some mutual sniffing, Spot gets to the point of the meeting. "Dick, did you pee on the Oval Office rug?" he asks, firmly. No answer. Spot grows agitated. *This is an important matter . . .* he thinks. *My VP shouldn't be ignoring me. This could bring down the entire administration.* He asks again. Nothing. It's as if Chewtoy can't hear him.

Wait a minute, Spot thinks. *Maybe he can't.*

Dick Chewtoy's one foot by one foot field of vision

Vice President Dick Chewtoy's safety head cone may have led to "political tunnel vision."

Realizing that Chewtoy is still wearing a cone fastened around his head to prevent him from chewing at his surgical stitches, Spot puts it all together. The cone, just by chance, is filtering out everything Dick Chewtoy doesn't want to see or hear. No wonder he's been so calm and content the last few days. Spot feels a tinge of jealousy.

CAT FANCY: SUPPORT FOR "WAR ON SQUIRRELS," "WAR ON CARS" ERODING

Dick Chewtoy may be calm, but adviser Karl Rover is getting increasingly nervous about Spot's numbers. Only 27 percent of the nation's dog lovers think the "War on Squirrels" is going well, and only 33 percent are happy with the progress on cars. The leak scandal will only erode these numbers further. Desperate, Rover remembers he'd heard a rumor that Dick Morris the Cat was unhappy with Mittens's refusal to leave his hiding spot to make public appearances.

On a hunch, he calls Morris (having his cell number because Morris actually consulted for the Dog Party in Spot's last election— Morris always goes wherever the Sheba is). Morris answers his cell, not particularly surprised by the call. They chat for *three* hours.

The next morning, the Pug Report posts a stunner.

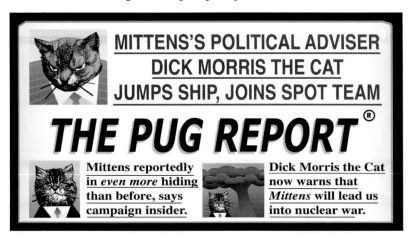

The Pug Report reveals that Dick Morris the Cat has joined the Spot campaign.

It's true. Mittens's political consultant, a serial turncat, has joined the competition midstream, leaving Mittens to fend for himself at the height of the growing Gennipurr Flowers scandal. Karl Rover has done it again. Can Mittens possibly recover?

More press roundup on the latest Spot, Mittens, Ishmael, and Polly election news.

New Ishmael, Polly Meet the Press

Only one day after his predecessor's death, Ishmael the V is sent out to convince a concerned press and public that this third-party candidate is still in the running. His updated campaign slogan, "Four More Hours," replaces Ishmael the IV's overly optimistic "Four More Weeks."

The new Ishmael (the V) joins the pet race.

Meanwhile, Polly, the Florida parrot, unveils his new slogan, the catchy "What *He* Said," at a rally in Palm Beach. Positioning himself as the "candidate who speaks for you, or at least *like* you" Polly draws thousands. This is one bird who's frightening a certain cat.

Mittens Looks for Morris Replacement

With Dick Morris the Cat's sudden defection to the Dog Party, Mittens has little time to dillydally on a replacement. With new competition and his upcoming nomination at the DemoCatic National Cat Show in North Smithfield, Rhode Island, only two weeks away, *he makes a call* to the only other adviser he knows that can pull a victory out of a cat.

He calls his old friend, a spit-filled Louisiana feline named James Catville.

9

SEPTEMBER

★ THE PET ★ CONVENTIONS

THE WESTMINSTER DOG AND KENNEL CONVENTION AND DEMOCATIC NATIONAL CAT SHOW

This year, the Westminster Dog and Kennel Convention is hosted in Chicago, winning bidder among competition from New York, San Francisco, and Dallas. Being a year in which the Dog Party has an incumbent running, the winner of "Best in Show" is a foregone conclusion, leaving the pet press with few surprises and no actual suspense to write about. For the most part, it's a giant infomercial for dogs, with an occasional pooping scandal.

Spot arrives at the Westminster Kennel Convention.

Some news: While traveling across the United States by paw over the last week to arrive here on the Saturday before the convention (as is tradition), Spot has reportedly suffered an unspecified leg injury that required surgery, resulting in his needing a head cone (much like Mr. Chewtoy's).

The Politics of Plastic Head Cones

The media is quick to pick up on the fact that *both* dogs on the ticket are now wearing head cones. *Are they attempting to block out reality?* It smells of Dick Morris the Cat strategy, I think to myself. And then, there he is, right behind Spot, orchestrating the whole arrival. I attempt to ask him for the reasons he left Mittens's team, but he pushes right past me without even a glance. I do notice that Rover follows right behind him, and he winks at me. Stealing the opposition's main strategy guy has clearly cheered old Karl.

Certainly the numbers are not cheering him. The two wars continue to erode Spot's popularity. But this dog show, with its twenty-four-hour television news coverage, provides a quick opportunity to get a "bump" in his approval rating. The star-studded speakers list should help.

Speaker Benji *as seen in* Bark Another Day.

Benji Arrives

Most of the pre-convention press buzz has predictably focused upon the Dog Party's celebrity speaker, well-known Spot supporter Benji the dog. His earlier films, marked by tearjerkers like *Benji* and *Benji Come Home*, have since given way to monosyllabic, action-fueled star vehicles like *Countdown to Benji* and *Benji: Bark Another Day*. His *politics* have taken a similar path, and his high Q ratings promise a future in government.

Rumors are spreading throughout the pet press corps that Benji is "having problems" with his young wife of two (fourteen) years, Natasha, a fiery cockapoo, over his serial carousing. With the inevitability of this year's Westminster nominee, the possibility of a celebrity dog getting himself into a sexual scandal is the only thing keeping the media awake. Not to disappoint, Benji is humping Larry King's leg by 7 p.m. that night.

The Pug Report shows Benji mounting Larry King's leg.

MONDAY NIGHT

Tonight's speaker, Spot's father Spike, has only one thing he needs to accomplish: He has to remind pet lovers across the nation that Spot is the son of, well, *him*, as in President Spike, the popular shepherd who successfully led the country through the long, patriotic "War on Mailmen" back in the early '80s (in response to several mailmen "going postal" in the Midwest in 1982).

Spike doesn't disappoint. Helped by a backdrop of black-and-white film reels of heroic dogs chasing terrified mail-delivering insurgents, he reminds voters that there was a point, even during the celebrated "War on Mailmen," when cats suggested that the postal workers were winning!

Ex-president Spike speaks on Monday.

It's true. Back in 1983, the Cat Party *did* question the "War on Mailmen" due to its huge cost (delays in mail delivery), but most agree now that the world would be a much darker place if mailmen had won. Of course, comparing that war to the current "War on Squirrels" is like comparing apples and acorns, but Spike's oratory skills and charisma distract the audience from his weak parallel. Come Thursday night, Spot may have a hard time topping him.

BENJI'S SPEECH ON TUESDAY NIGHT

On screen, Benji oozes brute sexuality (ask Larry King's leg). In wartime, animal lovers look for a pet who completely embodies *home security*. That said, Benji is much smaller in dog person than he appears on film, especially in his most recent action flick, *Benji: Timedog* (pre-dictably, he goes backward in time to prevent J. F. Kittedy's Bay of Pugs). But his diminu-tive size does not keep him from reaching for larger-than-life themes tonight.

His speech, titled "Kibbles, Bits, and the Bard," an often clunky mix of old-fashioned homilies and Shakespeare

Speaker Benji, smaller in person.

quotes (he is, after all, an actor), kills. He openly questions Mittens's ability to run the country from underneath a bed (a fair point) and mentions Ishmael's drinking problem (unfair—yes, he is a fish, but he *breathes* the stuff). Benji leaves to a standing ova-tion. But backstage, he is seen again embracing Larry King's leg, fanning rumors of an affair.

On Wednesday night, Vice President Dick Chewtoy is on stage

(still wearing his head cone) and takes little time to get to the meat of his text. Making no mention of the Finnish Spitzgerald leak investigation or the party's two faltering wars, Chewtoy asks if pet owners really think that a cat can be *trusted*. Quoting a hit piece by T. S. Eliot, the VP warns voters that all cats possess three names: *"One that you give them, one that other cats*

know, and one that is a secret to everyone but the cat itself." The crowd gasps.

Conveniently leaving out the fact that a pressured T. S. Eliot eventually admitted that his cat story was totally fabricated, the vice president, staring directly into the camera, calls for Mittens to reveal his third *secret* name (in the interest of full disclosure). Stunning TV.

Chewtoy quotes T. S. Eliot during his speech.

SPOT'S CLOSING NIGHT SPEECH

Chewtoy's T. S. Eliot line from last night is playing *big* in pet newspapers and blogs. Dick Morris the Cat is ecstatic, for it was his idea. Karl Rover strokes his back, and Morris's butt perks up proudly. But now, tonight, Spot must seal the deal—by adding a little *Lewis Carroll* to the mix.

At 9 p.m. sharp, he trots up onto the stage. His cone, still around his head, focuses him with a sort of political tunnel vision.

President Spot quotes Lewis Carroll.

With no distractions, Spot launches right into his Lewis Carroll diatribe, comparing Mittens to the Cheshire Cat *". . . who appears and disappears at will, whenever it's in his best interest."* He asks the audience if they've ever heard of a "Cheshire Dog." No? That's because dogs always stay if you tell them to stay. *And I will stay*, Spot promises, *if you want me to stay*. With that, he begins his run around the stage in a large circle so the delegates can get a

good look at him. After a few laps, a Westminster judge jumps up and presents Spot with the "Best in Show" award, citing his excellent eye-to-ear-to-snout ratio. Then Baha Men's "Who Let the Dogs Out" blasts from the hall's woofers as Spot and his family wave goodnight.

A Westminster judge checks Spot's posture.

THE DEMOCATIC NATIONAL CAT SHOW

After the enthusiastic reaction to the Westminster Dog Convention, Mittens's new adviser, James Catville, knows he'll have to pull off a miracle to better it. Fortunately, he's got one. Due to his business ties in Hollywood, he has access to *famed dog lover* and *Golden Girls* actress Betty White. Distraught over the Dog Party's endless "War on Squirrels," White has agreed to speak on Tuesday night, a major coup! But that's not all.

Political adviser James Catville and close Hollywood friend Betty White.

With only days until the DemoCatic National Cat Show, Mittens still hasn't come out from under his bed to pick a running mate. Catville has had a brainstorm. Why not ask . . . *Betty White*! Yes, she's a *Homo sapien*, but 1) *all* animal lovers across the nation adore her, 2) she's been high-profile in animal rights marches since 1922, and 3) she's *really* angry about Spot's faltering "War on Squirrels." She's even been labeled a *squirrel sympathizer* by Bill O'Rottweiler on his show in late August.

Wonkatt site announces Betty White news.

OPENING NIGHT SURPRISE

To guarantee maximum coverage, Catville waits until minutes before the DemoCatic National Cat Show to announce that White has joined the ticket. Within seconds, Mittens gets a spike in online polls. Pet pundits speculate that having White on the ticket guarantees that the Cat Party will take Florida, ground zero of *Golden Girls* fan base. Catville is *good*.

BETTY WHITE: "BARKING IS NOT A STRATEGY"

Alluding to the Westminster Dog and Kennel Convention's theme, "Who Let the Dogs Out," Betty White's emotional Tuesday night speech pleads for the Spot administration to *bring the dogs back in*. Citing recent reports that the war is actually attracting squirrels from other regions to come fight (a New Hampshire black squirrel was reportedly seen taunting dogs in Ohio), White, near tears, calls for the "Neo-Corgis" of the Dog Party to admit that their preemptive strategy has actually made backyard bird feeders *even more dangerous than before.* And then, as a woman, she challenges the Dog Party's bitches, specifically Corgileezza Rice, to rein in the alpha males of their pack.

Finally, White's last line, "Spot, bad dog . . . *bad dog*!" sends a chill down every canine's spine in America. The world's most beloved dog lover is angry at them. The world cannot ignore this.

The Dog Party's Corgileezza Rice was one of the targets of Betty White's ire.

MITTENS'S CLOSING NIGHT "APPEARANCE"

Still awash from the glow of Betty White's emotional star-turn on Tuesday night, James Catville has managed to convince Mittens to appear (!) on closing night—albeit from underneath a bed positioned on the main stage.

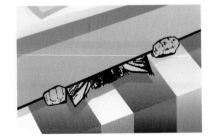

Though he doesn't technically *appear*, per se, Mittens's paw is visible occasionally as members of the crowd are allowed to dangle a string near his bed while Al Stewart's "Year of the Cat" blasts from the

Mittens's closing night "appearance."

sound system. It's the most anyone has seen of Mittens since the primaries, so it builds *some* hope.

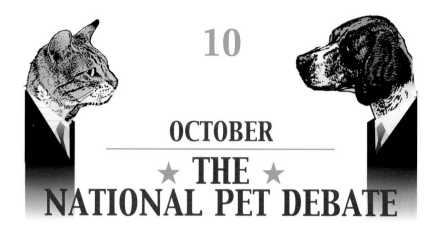

10

OCTOBER

★ THE ★
NATIONAL PET DEBATE

Whatever "bump" the Dog Party got from their convention was effectively erased by actress Betty White's stirring appearance at the DemoCatic National Cat Show on Tuesday night. Even Mittens's underwhelming Thursday night sort-of appearance doesn't seem to have tempered the surge in numbers the Cat Party is getting from the nation's *Golden Girls* elderly fan base.

But now, the true test awaits: the national pet debate.

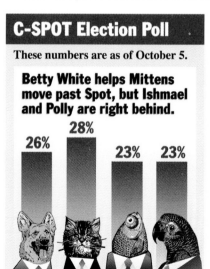

C-SPOT Election Poll

These numbers are as of October 5.

Betty White helps Mittens move past Spot, but Ishmael and Polly are right behind.

26% 28% 23% 23%

The election tightens up before the debate.

New candidates Ishmael and Polly's numbers continue to rise, so it's decided that both the goldfish and the parrot will be allowed to participate in the pet debate. The only question mark is whether Catville can convince Mittens to appear without cover.

MORRIS SCANDAL

Mere weeks after jumping on Spot's team, Dick Morris the Cat and his uncontrollable appetites are already starting to become a concern. The Fluffington Post, Arianna Fluffington's celebrity cat–addled online blog, is rumored to have obtained photos of Morris licking the back paws of a well-known Washington, D.C., call cat known as Cat Nip. Morris's paw fetish, well known in the local mating clubs, could lose Spot the few older dog lovers he hasn't already lost to beloved Betty White. Something must be done.

Arianna Fluffington's celebrity pet–addled Fluffington Post outs Morris's paw fetish.

DICK MORRIS THE CAT RESIGNS

"I've become too much of a distraction," an openly weeping Morris tells the press, "so I'm announcing my resignation so the focus of the debate will be on Spot's *ideas*, and not my own personal problems." Then, slightly perking up, he continues, "But I'd like to take advantage of the fact you're all here to announce that I've joined Ishmael the V's team, effective now." Morris then goes on to call Spot "a dog that could lead the country into nuclear war."

And with that, the four candidates begin to prepare for the event.

THE NATIONAL PET DEBATE—YPSILANTI, MICHIGAN

Perhaps the biggest surprise of this national pet debate is that political consultant James Catville has convinced Mittens to appear live, though again from under a bed positioned on the stage (with vague promises we may see *two* paws this time). The only off-limit topics are "persistent vomiting" and "licking oneself in front of company." Woof Blitzer and Catty Couric will ask the questions.

OFFICIAL DEBATE TRANSCRIPT

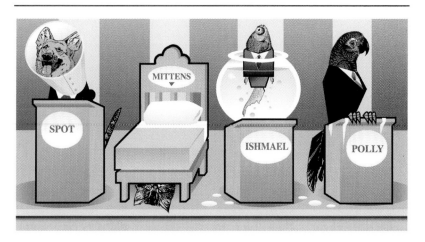

Spot, Mittens, Ishmael, and Polly at the national pet debate in Ypsilanti, Michigan

WOOF BLITZER: My first question is for Spot. Four months ago, you justified the "War on Cars" by claiming that automobiles were somehow linked to the squirrel attacks on our nation's backyard birdfeeders. Documents now show that you ignored experts within your own administration who tried to tell you that this was impossible due to the fact that squirrels and cars are natural enemies. Spot, can you explain?

SPOT: Woof, this has *always* been about *spreading* democracy through the world's backyards and motorways. Squirrels and cars have been fighting for generations over one little strip of road. If I can convince them to share that road, world peace is possible!

WOOF BLITZER: Wait a second . . . you just changed your story. Now you claim you're trying to bring squirrels and cars to the negotiation table? I thought you said the United States attacked squirrels and cars because they were a threat to our dog freedom.

SPOT: I never said that.

WOOF BLITZER: Yes, you did. On my show. I have the tape.

SPOT: [Pause.] Well . . . I only said it to confuse the enemy. If I had told the truth, I would have put many dogs' lives in danger. In fact, I'm lying *right now*, *again*, for that very same reason.

WOOF BLITZER: You're lying *now*? Which means you're lying about your previous lying about the reason? I'm confused.

SPOT: Exactly. I am *purposefully* confusing the enemy. [Applause.].

CATTY COURIC: This question is for Mittens. Is it true . . .
[Couric is interrupted by the sudden, violent sound of cat vomiting coming from under the bed.]
Mittens, are you throwing up? Are you all right?

MITTENS: That question's off-limits, that is so . . . [More sounds of vomiting.]

CATTY COURIC: [Flustered.] You're right, I'm sorry. Mittens, what was your reaction to South Dakota's recent total ban on spaying?

MITTENS: Before I answer than question, I just want to mention that Vice President Dick Chewtoy's daughter is a *Homo sapiens*. [Gasps in audience.] Not that there's anything wrong with that.

SPOT: [Angry.] That's *their* private family matter. She's a dog who just *thinks* she's a *Homo sapiens*. Many young dogs go through this phase. What does this have to do with Catty's question?

MITTENS: Apologies! I think I misheard. What was the ques . . .

SPOT: [Interrupts.] He purposely brought that up to rattle my base!

MITTENS: No, no! What dog owner hasn't suspected that their pet thinks it's a *Homo sapiens* at some point?! I brought it up out of the deepest sympathy! I would never exploit the *Homo sapienality* of an opponent's daughter just to get votes. Mr. Chewtoy's *Homo sapiens* daughter deserves better than that. What was the question?

CATTY COURIC: I . . . I don't remember . . . [Shuffles through notes.]

MITTENS: [To Spot.] Please apologize to Chewtoy's *Homo sapiens* daughter about this. I misheard the original question, I . . .

[Mittens proceeds to again mention Chewtoy's daughter's *Homo sapienality* fifty-three times over the next few minutes, which we have edited due to space limitations.]

Ishmael the V dies during national pet debate.

WOOF BLITZER: Enough! This one is for Ishmael. [Pause.] Ishmael?
[Blitzer notices that third-party pet candidate Ishmael the V is floating at the top of his bowl. He appears to have died.]

WOOF BLITZER: [To the television audience.] We're going to take a short break while Ishmael's team goes out to purchase a new goldfish. We apologize for the delay . . .

[The break lasts about forty-five minutes, as the closest pet store is in Ann Arbor. The new Ishmael is quickly named "Ishmael the VI." We resume with a question directed at Polly the Parrot.]

CATTY COURIC: Do believe in Dog?

POLLY THE PARROT: [Squawk.] Do you believe in Dog? [Squawk.].

CATTY COURIC: [Flustered.] This isn't about me; this is about you.

POLLY THE PARROT: This isn't about me, it's about you. [Squawk.] [Misinterpreting Polly's mimicking as his attempt to shed light on her own moral vacuum, Couric runs off the stage in tears. Filling in, Blitzer hurriedly directs a question at the new Ishmael.]

WOOF BLITZER: Um . . . Ishmael, what is your party's stand on right to life? Ishmael? Ishm . . . oh my God!
[Ishmael the VI is floating at the top of his bowl. It appears he has died again, this time during the Couric delay.]

SPOT: I'd say he's against it.

END OF DEBATE TRANSCRIPT

The debate is halted due to Ishmael's second death in five minutes. Predictably, the next day's sensationalistic news coverage of the debate focuses far more on the two third-party candidate deaths than on some of the important issues discusses therein. For those columnists and bloggers who did cover the issues, most found Spot and Mittens to be evasive. Everyone agreed that Polly the Parrot won the debate by default—and also for making Catty Couric cry. His numbers go up accordingly.

11

NOVEMBER

★ PET ★
ELECTION DAY

Only days before the national pet election, the newshound and alleged cat sympathizer Keith Dobermann leads off his cable news show with a report that Spot appeared to have a mysterious *bump* protruding from his back during the national pet debate two weeks ago. Speculation runs rampant, with pro-cat bloggers even suggesting that a radio transmitter was giving Spot his answers.

In public, Karl Rover, Spot's political adviser, laughs off the rumor, but behind the scenes he is working furiously to dispose of any evidence.

A TRANSMITTER OR A SEBACEOUS CYST?

A Washington veterinarian is hired to explain to the press that bumps discovered during debates are common on a dog Spot's age—and *harmless*.

Keith Dobermann on Spot's debate "bump."

Spot's Debate "Bump" Press Conference

The following is a transcript of the press conference in which White House veterinarian Dr. Larry explains Spot's bump.

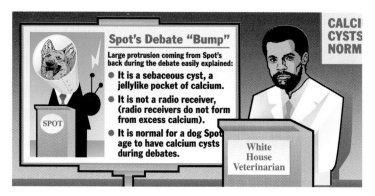

White House veterinarian tries to convince the press that Spot's bump is a calcium cyst.

DR. LARRY: Good evening. I'm here to report on the president's bump seen during the national pet debate. Spot's body was merely trying to expel toxins, which sometimes form calcium cysts that appear as large, jellylike bumps on a dog his age. This is what you all saw, nothing else.

WOOF BLITZER: But the bump had an antenna coming out of it.

DR. LARRY: That's perfectly normal for a dog his age. We've added three drops of liquid kelp to his daily diet to get rid of the antenna. No worries.

WOOF BLITZER: But witnesses have stated that static, followed by the words "Can you read me?" came out of this "calcium cyst."

DR. LARRY: Hmmm. Six drops of echinacea or goldenseal a day should get rid of that noise. We looked at it, and it's benign. But if the press notices any further bumps, certainly bring the president back in and we'll have a look. Thank you and good night.

[Dr. Larry exits the room, and the press is ushered out abruptly.]

The press conference does little to end speculation over the bump's origins, but the pet press is quickly distracted by another developing scandal, this time centering on Mittens.

The Mittens-Jane Fonda Photo: Altered?

Much like the Gennipurr Flowers revelation conveniently distracted from the Spot leak scandal, now a "found" photo linking Mittens to war activist Jane Fonda has surfaced to take attention away from Spot's bump. No one doubts that Karl Rover is behind these pictures, but the execution is surprisingly shoddy, suggesting that Spot's team is growing desperate about their prospects on November 2.

A doctored photo placing Mittens with Jane Fonda.

To begin with, putting Mittens (born in 1998) in a picture with Jane Fonda circa 1972 is just plain lazy. There is always the odd chance *60 Minutes* will do the math. But the follow-up

New photo places Mittens with Hitler, Cruise.

picture of Mittens standing alongside Adolf Hitler and Tom Cruise at a Nazi rally proves Rover's opinion of voters' IQs.

Oddly, Rover's ruse actually *works*. Even though animal lovers realize rationally that there is no possible way that Mittens posed with either Fonda, Hitler, or Cruise, they're still bothered by the fact that he would have allowed himself to pose for a picture that could so easily be doctored to include a Fonda or Hitler. Can a cat who can be so easily added into a damning photo possibly lead the country?

The Day Before Election Day

In a rather blatant attempt to reach out to Asian pet lovers, James Catville unveils a new Mittens slogan, "Hello Kitty, Hello Jobs," at a rally in Japantown, New York. With only one day remaining before the election, the Cat Party is desperate to shed Mittens's Flowers, Fonda, and Hitler baggage with the upbeat message of job growth.

Across the nation, the newly purchased Ishmael, now the VII (I think), is pressing the flesh in San Diego, a conservative Dog Party stronghold. Spot's recent scandals have made the sunny city up for grabs.

News coverage on November 1, the day before election.

Polly Wants a Scandal

It was only a matter of time before Polly's string of luck ran out. The Dog Party, Cat Party, and Ishmael (well, actually his new adviser, Dick Morris the Cat) were working overtime to dig up dirt in the parrot's past, and Morris found it in a statement Polly made in 2000 to a previous owner. When asking for a favorite snack, Polly allegedly proclaimed, "Polly wants a cracker." It went unnoticed at the time, but with the spotlights of a national pet election upon him, these words would take on a new, *racist* resonance. Dick Morris the Cat would make sure of it.

DID POLLY MAKE RACIST 'CRACKER' COMMENT IN 2000?

WAS REQUEST FOR FOOD ACTUALLY AN ATTACK ON NEARBY WHITE PERSON?

THE PUG REPORT ®

Nearby white person: "I was scared for my life. He was so mean . . ."

MORRIS: Racist Polly will lead us into nuclear war . . .

Polly — Full of hate?

The Pug Report posts Polly's late-in-the-game scandal.

POLLY DENIES ALLEGED RACIST REMARK

Faced with accusations that his alleged request for food in 2000 was in fact an overt confession that he prefers *white voters* over black voters, Polly issues a statement by his former owner, who says that Polly is "the least racist parrot I've ever met in my life." But by now the pet press is picking over his past, looking for any other examples of his alleged xenophobia. Polly supporters' defense—that he might have mimicked racist remarks to shed light on their inherent absurdity—fails to stick. Fortunately for Polly, the political opera-

Damage control on Woof.

tive who created this whole scandal will, within moments, have a new scandal of his own. And this is one scandal he and his client won't survive.

ISHMAEL: IN THE BELLY OF THE BEAST

Though Dick Morris the Cat's kinky sexual appetite has been covered at length in this book, another appetite of his is sometimes forgotten: his stomach's. According to online news source Wonkatt, Morris, in a drunken, out-of-control binge, had mistakenly scooped Ishmael the VII out of his goldfish bowl late last night *and eaten him.* With no memory of the event, Morris found pieces of fin in his bed this morning. Devastated by his actions, he resigns and hides under a bed.

With no more goldfish available at the local pet store, Ishmael is effectively out of the race, leaving a dog, a cat, and a parrot as the only pets left vying to lead our country.

Ishmael's followers throw their support to Polly. The surge puts the parrot at a dead heat with Spot and Mittens, all at 32 percent.

Wonkatt breaks the latest Morris the Cat scandal.

ELECTION DAY, 4 P.M.

After eleven exhausting months, it all comes down to today. Spot, Mittens, and Polly make a few final, last-minute campaign stops, but by 4 p.m., all three are huddled inside each of their campaign headquarters to watch the night's results with family.

Of course, the best place to gauge the early vote is the Internet. Wonkatt and the Fluffington Post both post hopeful numbers for Mittens, based on the inexact science of exit polling. A smiling James Catville is in the corner poring over every election blog he can find. Mittens might take Florida, according to the blogs Daily Kat and Catrios. This would be pretty huge (thank Betty White). But it's way too early to break out the cream.

6 P.M.: VOTER FRAUD RUMORS IN FLORIDA, OHIO

Some stories begin to surface that irregularities are occurring in several Midwestern states. One rumor puts a *double-pawed* Angora in charge of counting ballots in Ohio (a sure sign of a miscount). It proves to be false.

Another rumor that appears to be false, proves to be true. Polly, the parrot pet candidate, is making a strong showing in several dog states. In fact, the Norwegian Blue is tied with Mittens in Florida!

THE FLUFFINGTON POST

DELIVERING NEWS AND OPINION

THE NEWS   THE BLOG   CONTAGIOUS FESTIVAL

MITTENS LEADING WITH ONE VOTE IN . . . (Comments)

At current rate, Mittens will totally win . . . (Comments)

Mittens, projected winner!!!

Tough-luck loser Lassie: "Wait, only one vote is in." (Comments)

Projected Result At Current Rate

With one vote in, Mittens is projected to get all possible votes.*
*No margin of error.

■ Spot
■ Mittens
□ Polly
▲ N

Optimistic exit poll numbers on Fluffington Post.

8 P.M.: EARLY CAT PARTY LEAD SHRINKING

Mittens's early leads in Florida, Ohio, and Vermont are starting to evaporate. Polly actually passes Mittens in Florida, a stunning development considering the Betty White factor. The actress is close to tears, realizing her national influence has been weakened by nonstop *Golden Girls* rerun saturation over the last decade. It's also becoming obvious that Mittens's refusal to come out from under his bed was a major factor in this race.

Spot and clan follow the results on C-SPOT.

10 P.M.—DOG STATES TAKEN BY PARROT

Even Spot is now hiding under a bed. Florida, Texas,

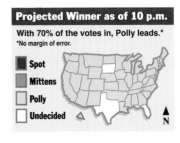

Projected Winner as of 10 p.m.

With 70% of the votes in, Polly leads.*
*No margin of error.

- Spot
- Mittens
- Polly
- Undecided   △   ▲ N

Electoral map: Dog, cat states are going to parrot.

Voting Closed, Parrot Sweeps

With 100% of the votes in, Polly wins.*
*No margin of error.

- Spot
- Mittens
- Polly

Electoral College
Polly - 538 votes
Spot - 0 votes
Mittens - 0 votes   △   ▲ N

The electoral map shows Polly sweeping.

Ohio, and South Dakota have gone to Polly. Exit polls reveal a deep malaise in the country over the wars on squirrels and cars. And the leak scandal has eroded faith that the Dog Party is willing to wait to go pee outside the White House. (Though exit polls also show that most pet owners think a cat would pee on the Oval Office rug, too. This is telling.)

HUGE UPSET?

Though still too early to call, Woof Blitzer is the first to speculate that the next pet president of the United States will be Polly, a parrot. Most news stations refrain from naming a winner until the next morning, despite the election's lopsided results. But Woof would be right.

THE DAY AFTER—WINNERS AND LOSERS

Though one look at the pet election's electoral map shows a clear Polly victory (the parrot candidate took all fifty states *and* the popular vote 122,293,563 to Spot's 2 and Mittens's 1), both Spot and Mittens ask for a recount. The Cat Party even suggests that pet owners with black cats were kept from voting in Florida. But a recount shows the final numbers *even more* in favor of the parrot: Polly: 122, 293,565; Spot: 1; Mittens: 0. (He hadn't even left his hiding spot to vote for himself.) The next day, the nation's headlines announce a new pet president.

The DemoCat & Chronicle *headline announces the new United States pet president.*

PET ELECTION ANALYSIS AND AFTERMATH

"Animals are such agreeable friends—they ask no questions,
they pass no criticisms."
—George Eliot (Secret third cat name: Mary Ann Evans)

Months have passed since the shocking results of this historic pet election. In January, Polly the Parrot was sworn in (his mimicking skills came in quite handy here). Spot has retreated to his Texas doghouse (he's rumored to be licking again). Mittens has gone missing, which he almost already was, anyway. An eighth Ishmael was finally purchased in Ann Arbor and is said to be considering a run against Polly in four years (if he makes it).

What have we learned? Perhaps the most revealing aspect of this election's results was pet lovers' total loss of faith in the classic Dog and Cat Party system. So low was their regard for these two animals that they knowingly elected a bird, who merely repeats what you say but never means it.

Is the parrot the pet leader of our future? Will parrots inspire us to reach beyond ourselves, to make the future a better one for our children and pets? Only time will tell.

★ EPILOGUE ★

A few months after author Don Asmussen handed in this manuscript, a popular Web site called TheSmokingPug.com openly questioned the validity of much of his information (which Asmussen had previously published in many articles for *Dog & Cat Quarterly*). The site claimed that Asmussen *was never an investigative reporter* and that no such national pet election ever took place. Other critics have suggested that several passages from this book are "strikingly similar" to passages in John Grogan's best-selling pet book *How Marley & Me Got Licked, Got Wild, and Got a Life.* When confronted, Asmussen ran under a bed. Lawsuits are still pending.